STAR ☆ FILES

Beyoncé Knowles

Nicola Hodgson

www.raintreepublishers.co.uk
Visit our website to find out more information about **Raintree** books.

To order:
☎ Phone 44 (0) 1865 888113
▤ Send a fax to 44 (0) 1865 314091
💻 Visit the Raintree Bookshop at **www.raintreepublishers.co.uk** to browse our catalogue and order online.

 Produced for Raintree by
White-Thomson Publishing Ltd
Bridgewater Business Centre
210 High Street, Lewes, BN7 2NH

First published in Great Britain by Raintree,
Halley Court, Jordan Hill, Oxford OX2 8EJ,
part of Harcourt Education.
Raintree is a registered trademark of
Harcourt Education Ltd.

Editorial: Catherine Clarke, Sarah Shannon and
Kate Buckingham
Design: Leishman Design and Michelle Lisseter
Picture Research: Catherine Clarke
Production: Chloe Bloom

Originated by Modern Age
Printed and bound in China by South China
Printing Company

ISBN 1 844 43296 3
09 08 07 06 05
10 9 8 7 6 5 4 3 2 1

**British Library Cataloguing in
Publication Data**
Hodgson, Nicola.
Beyoncé Knowles. – (Star Files)
782.4'21643'092
A full catalogue record for this book is
available from the British Library.

Acknowledgements
The publishers would like to thank the following
for permission to reproduce photographs:
Allstar pp. **8** (l) (Cinetext Collection), **15** (r)
(Cinetext Collection), **19** (Allstar Collection), **25** (t)
(Cinetext Collection), **26** (Cinetext Collection), **27**
(l) (Cinetext Collection), **27** (r), **30** (Allstar
Collection), **38** (Allstarpl.com), **39** (r)
(Allstarpl.com), **41** (r) (Allstar Collection), **42** (r)
(Allstar Collection); Corbis pp. **4** (Frank Trapper),
6, **22** (l), **23** (Ethan Miller), **28** (r) (Neville Elder),
31 (Frank Trapper), **32** (Reuters), **37** (t) (Reuters);
Getty Images (PhotoDisc) pp. **14**, **25** (b), **33** (r);
Harcourt Education Ltd p. **13** (r) (Gareth Boden);
Retna p. **11**; Retna Ltd pp. **5** (Cookie Rosenberg), **7**
(l) (Tammie Arroyo/AFF), **7** (r) (Sara De Boer) **12**
(Elgin Edmonds), **13** (l) (Jeff Slocomb), **15** (l) (John
Spellman), **21** (John Spellman), **24** (Walter
McBride) **39** (l) (Gina James/Graylock.com); Retna
UK (Jack Cousin) p. **10**; Rex Features pp. **8** (r)
(Albert Ferreira), **9** (Alex Berliner), **16** (Jim Smeal),
17 (Brian Rasic), **18** (Dave Lewis), **20** (Jim Smeal),
22 (r) (Brian Rasic), **28** (l) (Brian Rasic), **29** (Sylvain
Gaboury), **33** (l) (Julian Makey), **34** (Bill Davila),
35 (r) (Matt Baron), **35** (l) (Tim Rooke), **36** (Dave
Allocca), **37** (b) (Dezo Hoffmann), **40** (Brian Rasic),
41 (l) (S. Gaboury), **42** (l) (Richard Young), **43** (Ray
Tang). Cover photograph reproduced with
permission of Corbis (Frank Trapper).

Quote sources: pp. **4**, **7**, **8**, **9**, **10**, **13**, **14**, **16**, **17**,
19, **22**, **24**, **25**, **26**, **27**, **34**, **35**, **39**, **42** *Soul
Survivors, the Official Autobiography of Destiny's
Child*, Beyoncé Knowles, Kelly Rowland and
Michelle Williams, with James Patrick Herman;
pp. **39** *Destiny's Style – Bootylicious Fashion, Beauty,
and Lifestyle Secrets from Destiny's Child*, Tina
Knowles with Zoe Alexander; pp. **33** *Beyoncé*,
Kathleen Tracy; pp. **20**, **29**, **31**, **32**, **33**, **43**
interview in *Observer Music Monthly*, 14 December
2003; pp. **21** liveDaily Interview with Michelle
Williams, Colin Devenish; pp. **24** Internet Movie
Database; pp. **31** www.grammy.com; pp. **33**
www.beatboxbetty; pp. **33** interview on
www.abcnews.com June 4 2004; pp. **32** *The Mirror*,
8 July 2003; pp. **34** www.childrenfirst.nhs.uk;
pp. **41** talklivedaily.com 8 November 2003; pp. **41**
www.killermovies.com.

The publishers would like to thank Rosie Nixon,
Charly Rimsa and Marie Lorimer for their assistance
in the preparation of this book.

Contents

Any words appearing in the text in bold, **like this**, are explained in the glossary. You can also look out for them in the Star words box at the bottom of each page.

Say her name!

ALL ABOUT BEYONCÉ

Full name: Beyoncé Giselle Knowles
Born: 4 September 1981
Place of birth: Houston, Texas, USA
Height: 1.67 metres (5 feet 6 inches)
Relationships: Boyfriend: Jay-Z
Big break: Destiny's Child appeared on the soundtrack to *Men in Black* in 1997
Interests: song writing, painting, fashion, swimming, exercising
Family: Father: Mathew, mother: Tina, younger sister: Solange

Beyoncé Knowles is young, rich, talented, and famous. She is one of the most popular performers in the world. She also knows just how lucky she is. She tries to stay down to earth. She says, "I'm blessed. I used to dream about achieving this level of success … There are so many people out there who want to be in my shoes."

Star words   producer person that decides how a song will sound when it is being recorded

Many talents

Not everyone realized how talented Beyoncé was. They said she was just a pretty girl who got lucky. It takes more than looks to be a pop star, though. Beyoncé is a fantastic singer and dancer. She writes songs and is a record **producer**. She has also acted in films and runs her own fashion business.

Staying focused

Beyoncé also knows how much hard work it takes to succeed in the music business. She started performing when she was just 7 years old. She kept working and stayed focused. It has not always been easy. There have been a lot of setbacks and hard times, too. She has managed to overcome them and come back stronger each time.

Beyoncé is now famous for her amazing singing voice.

Find out later

Who were the girls in the first Destiny's Child line-up?

How many Grammy awards did Beyoncé win in 2004?

Who worked with Beyoncé on her first solo album?

Starting out

Unique name

Beyoncé has an unusual name. It is actually her mother Tina's **maiden name**. Tina was very close to her own mother, Agnes. She wanted a way of passing her mother's name to her own daughter. Beyoncé's friends and family often call her by the nickname "Bee".

Beyoncé was born on 4 September 1981 at Park Plaza Hospital in Houston, Texas, USA. Her father Mathew was a salesman. Her mother Tina worked in a bank. Later, when she had saved enough money, Tina opened her own hair salon. This had always been her dream.

Both Beyoncé's parents worked very hard. Mathew was a top salesman and Tina's hair salon became very successful. This taught Beyoncé an important lesson when she was growing up. If you want to achieve something, you have to keep trying and you have to work hard.

Beyoncé was born in Houston, Texas.

Star words inherit passed down from your parents or grandparents

The shy girl

Beyoncé was a shy and quiet little girl. She got nervous if her teachers asked her anything. She says that she was chubby and often felt self-conscious. She dressed like a tomboy. Beyoncé studied hard and was well behaved in school, but felt that she did not fit in with the other kids. Then she found something that made her feel good: she loved to sing and dance.

> ❝ Both my parents were always working, and I inherited my drive to succeed from them. ❞

Beyoncé and her sister Solange.

Beyoncé is often seen out with her parents.

Solange Knowles

Beyoncé's younger sister Solange has been a back-up dancer for her. She is also a singer, and released an album called *Solo Star* in 2003. Solange is married to an American-football player called Daniel Smith. They have a son who is also called Daniel.

maiden name woman's surname before she is married

Child star

Beyoncé says that she loved music from the start. She would learn songs at school and then come home and sing them for her mother. She started taking dance lessons when she was seven. Her parents thought it would be a way for their shy daughter to make new friends. Her teacher, Miss Darlett, soon saw that her new student had real talent. She said that Beyoncé should try performing at local talent shows.

As a baby, I would go crazy whenever I heard music, and I tried to dance before I could even walk.

Houston stars

Beyoncé is not the only celebrity from Houston. Oscar-winning actress Renée Zellweger is from the Houston suburb of Katy. Singer and actress Hilary Duff also grew up in the city. Renée Zellweger (above) showed that she could act, sing, and dance in the film *Chicago*.

Beyoncé feels at home on stage.

Star words

audition chance for a musician or actor to perform to see if they are right to join a group or get a part

Talent shows

Beyoncé appeared in her first talent show when she was 7 years old. She sang John Lennon's song "Imagine". Her parents came to watch her sing. They were amazed at how well she did. Beyoncé remembers how she felt: "I felt at home on that stage, more so than anywhere else." Even today, she says that she feels **transformed** when she is performing.

Beyoncé with one of her favourite singers – Diana Ross.

Award winner

Beyoncé carried on taking part in competitions and beauty **pageants**. Her bedroom was full of trophies and awards. Her parents supported her, but did not force her to compete. Beyoncé says, "I wasn't forced into this lifestyle … my parents never insisted that I perform in talent shows."

Being spotted

When Beyoncé was 10 years old, some music **managers** spotted her at a talent show. They asked Beyoncé to come to an **audition** for an all-girl group that they were setting up. This group was called Girl's Tyme. It was here that Beyoncé would first meet the girls who became Destiny's Child.

Beyoncé's favourite singers

Aaliyah
Anita Baker
Aretha Franklin
Diana Ross
Janet Jackson
Mariah Carey
Michael Jackson
Whitney Houston

manager   person that takes care of the business side of running a pop group

Girl's Tyme

The group that Beyoncé first joined – Girl's Tyme – performed at local events. It was through Girl's Tyme that Beyoncé met two of the girls who went on to become Destiny's Child. First of all, Beyoncé met LaTavia Roberson. A short while later, Kelly Rowland joined Girl's Tyme. There were six girls in the group. They were all 10 or 11 years old.

> We rehearsed all the time. Even when we were only 10 years old!
> (Kelly Rowland)

Another sister

The group practised every day. Kelly and Beyoncé enjoyed performing together. They became close friends. Kelly's mother was a single mum who was having a hard time. Beyoncé's father Mathew suggested that Kelly move in with the Knowles family. She and Beyoncé shared a room. Beyoncé says that at first it was hard sharing, but then Kelly became like another sister.

Star Search

In 1992, when Beyoncé was 11 years old, Girl's Tyme got a chance to go on *Star Search*. This was a television talent show. The girls hoped that this would be their big break.

Star words   devastated very sad and upset

Kelly Rowland

Kelly Rowland lived with Beyoncé's family from the age of ten. Later, Mathew became her **legal guardian**. Kelly says that she thinks of Mathew and Tina as being second parents to her.

★ ★ ★ ★ ★ ★ ★ ★ ★ ★

Mathew has been like a father to Kelly (left).

They **rehearsed** every day for months. They tried really hard, but they lost. The girls were **devastated**. Then they made a difficult decision. They were going to carry on, and they were going to work harder than ever before.

legal guardian someone who is not your real parent, but who is responsible for looking after you

Children of destiny

★ ★ ★ ★ ★ ★ ★ ★ ★ ★ ★

Changing names

The girls tried out different names for their group. First they were Girl's Tyme, then Somethin' Fresh, then Borderline, then Cliché, then The Dolls. After that, they tried Destiny. It was Beyoncé's dad, Mathew, who finally suggested the name Destiny's Child.

Mathew saw how serious Beyoncé and the other girls were about the group. He decided to help them by getting more involved. Girl's Tyme broke up, but the girls formed a new group, with Mathew as their **manager**. There were four girls in the new group. LaTavia, Kelly, and Beyoncé stayed. In 1993, a school friend of Beyoncé's, LeToya Luckett, also joined. This was the line-up that would become Destiny's Child.

By this time, Beyoncé was going to Houston's High School for the Performing and Visual Arts. On top of all her school work, she was **rehearsing** with the group. Sometimes the girls practised for 8 hours a day.

The original Destiny's Child.

Star words   committed   very serious about something

Beyoncé's family is very important to her.

Working it

Beyoncé decided that she wanted to get healthy. She says it was very difficult to see the other girls eating pizza and ice cream when she was eating soup and low-fat foods. She also went jogging every day.

Family troubles

Mathew really believed in the girls. He even decided to leave his job so that he could be the girls' full-time manager. He could see how **committed** they were. Sadly, all the work he put into managing the girls ended up damaging his marriage. When Beyoncé was 14 years old, her parents separated.

> He wanted to make our dreams come true, and he saw that magic in us. (Beyoncé on her father)

In 1995, after all the hard work and the unhappy times, there was some good news. The girls got their first record deal. Beyoncé's parents worked out their problems and got back together.

No pizza for Beyoncé – she was being healthy!

13

The audition

Destiny's Child had to sing for the Columbia Records **executives** in a tiny office packed with people. It was a scary experience. They had no music or microphones and had to sing **a cappella**. Luckily, the executives liked what they heard.

The girls went to New York for their Columbia Records audition.

Breaking through

In 1995, when Beyoncé was 14 years old, Destiny's Child got a record deal. Daryl Simmons signed them to Silent Partner Productions. When they were signed, the girls moved to Atlanta. That was where the record company was based. LaTavia's mother was their **chaperone**, but otherwise the girls were all alone. They lived together in the basement of Daryl's assistant's house. They had lessons in the morning with a tutor. They spent the rest of the day in the studio. Beyoncé remembers this as a happy time. "We finally had a taste of independence," she says. They were getting some money from the record company, and they loved to shop!

> It was all about having a little bit of cash and a lot of freedom.

Star words

chaperone person who looks after and supervises younger people

Big break

Destiny's Child got their first real taste of success with their song "Killing Time". This song was part of the soundtrack for the film Men in Black, which starred Will Smith and Tommy Lee Jones (below).

Another setback

The girls soon found out that having a record deal does not mean that you have made it. After only 8 months, Silent Partner dropped the group. The girls had to start all over again. They were very disappointed, but Mathew tried to keep them positive. He was still working hard to make sure that they were noticed. Before long, he got the girls a chance to **audition** with Columbia Records in New York. It worked – the group was signed in 1996.

executive business person

Musical help

A lot of talented musicians helped Destiny's Child with their first album. Wyclef Jean **produced** some of their songs. The girls also worked with Jermaine Dupri. He is a famous record producer who has also worked with Usher, TLC, and Lil Bow Wow.

The first album

Destiny's Child were signed to Columbia Records in 1996. Their first album, simply called *Destiny's Child*, did not come out until 1998. They spent 2 years making sure that the sound was exactly right. "It was our **debut** album and we wanted it to be perfect," explains Kelly. Also, the girls were still getting an education. They left school when they were 14 years old. From then on, tutors taught them. This meant that they had very little spare time. When they were not taking lessons with their tutors, they were recording their album.

★ Star fact

"No, No, No" sold three million copies in the United States.

On the radio

Beyoncé was sixteen when Destiny's Child had their first hit with the song "No, No, No". She remembers hearing it on the radio one day when she was picking her sister up from school. Kelly was in the car with her, too. When the song came on, Beyoncé, Kelly, and Solange were so excited, they ran around the car shouting and singing along.

Jermaine Dupri has also worked with Janet Jackson – one of Beyoncé's favourite singers.

Star words   debut first

Not quite right?

Not everything was right with the album. The girls wanted people to notice them, but they realize now that they tried out too many different sounds. Kelly says, "We ended up with too many sounds... That didn't put us in a specific category or make us seem unique. It only made people confused." The album sold well. It sold half a million copies in 6 months. This was a good start, but Destiny's Child's second album would do much better.

Tina Knowles helped Destiny's Child with their "look" and matching outfits.

Destiny's style

Beyoncé's mother, Tina, became the **stylist** of Destiny's Child. She knew she could design clothes that suited the girls' personalities and make them look fantastic. Tina still works with Beyoncé as a solo artist, making her stage outfits.

stylist person who gives advice on hair, clothes, and make-up

The writing's on the wall

Bills, Bills, Bills

Beyoncé says that a lot of people did not get "Bills, Bills, Bills". The song is about a man who uses her money instead of paying his own way. Some people thought the song was about women using men for money. In the song "Independent Women Part 1" Beyoncé makes her ideas clear: "I pay my own bills."

Destiny's Child started working on their second album straight away. *The Writing's on the Wall* was released in July 1999. The single "Bills, Bills, Bills" came out in the same month. It was a huge hit. Now the girls felt that they were really getting somewhere. People loved them. They were selling records and getting a lot of attention. The album sold 1 million copies in just 2 months.

Things were going well for Destiny's Child – they were already winning awards.

A step forward

The album was an important step forward for Beyoncé. It was the first time that she tried writing songs and even **producing**. This was an amazing achievement for a young woman who was still only 17 years old. Everyone working on the album could see how talented she was.

> " Success is the real test of a friendship. "

The split

Just when they were becoming successful, the group faced their biggest setback yet. There had been problems between LeToya and LaTavia and the rest of the group for a while. In January 2000 things got so bad that LeToya and LaTavia decided to leave the group. One of the reasons they gave was that, because Mathew was Beyoncé's father, he favoured her over the other members. Beyoncé was **devastated** when she heard the news. Nobody was sure whether the group could carry on.

Beyoncé sang and acted in the film *The Fighting Temptations.*

Soundtracks

Songs by both Beyoncé and Destiny's Child have appeared on lots of film soundtracks:

Men in Black
Why Do Fools Fall in Love
The Best Man
Romeo Must Die
Charlie's Angels
Austin Powers in Goldmember
Bad Boys 2
The Fighting Temptations.

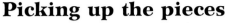

Michelle Williams

Michelle (below) had already toured the world when she was working as a back-up singer. She had not set out to be a singer, though. First of all she went to college to study. She had wanted to join the FBI!

Picking up the pieces

Beyoncé was very upset when LeToya and LaTavia left the group. After all, they had known each other since they were children and had been close friends for years. She went into a **depression** and stayed in her bedroom for weeks. Because of all the stress, her skin broke out in spots. She had such bad acne that she had to see a **dermatologist**.

Blaming Beyoncé

Suddenly, the **media** were interested in the group. Stories were coming out accusing Beyoncé of being a **diva**. They said that she wanted to be the leader of the group and wanted all the attention. Beyoncé remembers: "I had hate websites, and a lot of pressure, and people blaming everything on me." She was still only 18 years old. This was a lot for her to deal with.

The new line-up

While Beyoncé was coping with her loss, Mathew was busy trying to find two new girls to replace LeToya and LaTavia. He did not have long. The group was doing a lot of **promotional work** at the time. The song "Say My Name" was coming out as a single. They had only 2 weeks before they needed to shoot the video for the song. They held **auditions** and chose two new singers to join them: Michelle Williams and Farrah Franklin.

Star words

media types of communication such as television, radio, newspapers, and magazines

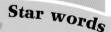

One of the group

Michelle says that she was made to feel one of the group straight away. "It was so cool, because they came and got me from the airport, I stayed at their house, I had a ball. We went to a seafood restaurant. We had so, so, so much fun. It turned out that I became one of the group, and I shot the video [for "Say My Name"] maybe a week or two after my audition."

Now Beyoncé is happy to answer questions at press conferences like this one.

The new line-up

The new-look Destiny's Child came out with the video for "Say My Name". LeToya and LaTavia sing on the song, but Michelle and Farrah **lip-synch** to their voices in the video. The new girls had just 2 days to learn the dance routine before filming the video. All the news about the changes in the group meant that the song got a lot of **publicity**. The song was another big hit for the girls. A few months later, in May 2000, they had more success with the single "Jumpin, Jumpin". By this time, the album *The Writing's on the Wall* had sold millions of copies.

A sudden split

Farrah left the group suddenly. The girls were going to Sydney, Australia (above), to perform. Beyoncé, Kelly, and Michelle were waiting for Farrah at the airport. Beyoncé got a phone call from her. She was not coming to Sydney. They never performed with Farrah again.

Another setback

Just when it seemed that things were going smoothly again, there was another setback. After only 5 months in the group, Farrah decided to leave. The girls had a very tough schedule. The new members had to work particularly hard to learn the songs and the dance routines. Farrah soon had enough.

The new line-up for Destiny's Child.

Star words   lip-synch   mime the words to a song rather than singing them

Down to three

Beyoncé could not believe what was happening. Once again, the future of the group was in danger. What were they going to do? It would be very different with just three members in the group. They decided to carry on. They would come back stronger than ever.

> We never would have been this popular if our member changes did not happen.

Better as three

When Destiny's Child appeared as a threesome for the first time, they were very nervous. They had to rework all their songs and dance routines in very little time. They found that something special had happened, though. Beyoncé says, "We sounded better than ever. It was just magical."

Who would have guessed that the group would be better as three?

publicity attention from newspapers, magazines, television and radio shows

23

Survivors

★ ★ ★ ★ ★ ★ ★ ★ ★ ★

Body image

Beyoncé says she wrote "Bootylicious" because "I had gained some weight and the pressure that people put you under, the pressure to be thin, is unbelievable. I was just eighteen and you shouldn't be thinking about that. You should be thinking about building up your character and having fun."

★ ★ ★ ★ ★ ★ ★ ★ ★ ★

Destiny's Child were more popular than ever as a three-girl group. They were asked to **contribute** a song to the soundtrack of the film *Charlie's Angels*. The film starred Cameron Diaz, Drew Barrymore, and Lucy Liu as three beautiful, but tough, detectives. The action-packed film was very successful, and the song "Independent Women Part 1" was another big hit for Destiny's Child.

> Writing songs is something that I was meant to do.

Back to the studio

After everything that had happened, Beyoncé was keen to get back into the studio. She says, "I wanted to write lyrics that expressed everything that Kelly, Michelle and I had been through together." It was a good year for Destiny's Child. The album *Survivor* came out in May 2001. Beyoncé **produced** most of the songs on it. She made the decisions about how these songs would sound – and she did a great job! The singles "Survivor", "Bootylicious", and "Emotion" were all big hits for the group. In October, they released a holiday album, *8 Days of Christmas*.

Being beautiful comes naturally to Beyoncé!

Star words   **ASCAP** American Society of Composers, Authors, and Publishers

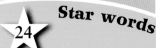

Charlie's Angels are "independent women".

The next challenge

After all that hard work, the girls were ready to take a break. They wanted to have a rest, but also to try some solo work. This led to rumours in the **media** that the group was splitting up. Beyoncé ignored the stories. She wanted to try some solo work, too. She also had another challenge in front of her. She was going to try acting.

★ Star fact

In 2002, Beyoncé was named Songwriter of the Year by **ASCAP**. She was the youngest person ever to win this award, the first African American, and only the second woman.

Beyoncé is not just a talented singer, she writes great songs, too.

I'm a survivor

One of the most popular songs that Beyoncé has written is "Survivor". She says, "I have met hundreds of children who are suffering from cancer and they always sing it to me … They are so strong, and seeing them gives me strength."

contribute give

Acting

Beyoncé's first acting job came in 2001. She was offered the lead part in an MTV production, *Carmen: A Hip Hopera*. This was a hip-hop version of the famous opera *Carmen*. The songs would be rapped rather than sung. Beyoncé was nervous about it. She had never acted before. She had never rapped before, either. The character she was playing was not at all like her. Beyoncé describes Carmen as "a **devious** and shady lady".

> There should always be something new in life that you're trying to do.

Foxxy was based on characters such as Coffy played by Pam Grier in the 1970s.

Star words   devious dishonest

Hollywood calls

Beyoncé's big break in acting came when she was offered a part in the third Austin Powers film, *Austin Powers in Goldmember*. She had to **audition** for the part. She met Mike Myers, the star and writer of the films, and Jay Roach, the **director**. She says she was very nervous, but they liked her and gave her the role. She had a lot to learn. She has never had any acting training and admits, "I have no idea what film people are talking about half the time."

Foxxy Cleopatra

Beyoncé plays Austin's sidekick Foxxy Cleopatra. Beyoncé liked playing Foxxy. She says, "I can relate a lot to her, because she's really strong and sassy and she has got a lot of soul."

Pam Grier became famous as the sassy Coffy.

Pam Grier

The character of Foxxy Cleopatra was partly based on the parts that the actress Pam Grier (above) had played. She became famous in the 1970s and is still a star today. Beyoncé watched a lot of Pam Grier films while she was preparing to play Foxxy Cleopatra.

director   person in charge of making a film

Going solo

Beyoncé with Jay-Z.

It was not long before Beyoncé returned to her first love, music. She started working on her first solo album in 2002. It was called *Dangerously in Love* and was released in June 2003.

A lot of people wondered how successful Beyoncé would be on her own. She soon showed them. *Dangerously in Love* turned her into a megastar.

Working with Jay-Z

Rap star Jay-Z features on "Crazy in Love". Beyoncé in turn had sung on his hit "03 Bonnie & Clyde". This song also appears on Beyoncé's solo album. The two stars had started dating around this time. There were rumours that they were engaged.

Beyoncé became a huge solo success.

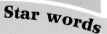
Star words   apologize say that you are sorry for something

Crazy right now

The biggest song on the album was "Crazy in Love". It was a massive hit for Beyoncé all around the world. She explains how she came to write it. The **producer**, Rich Harrison, already had an idea for the music. They needed to write some lyrics. When she met him, she says she was looking scruffy. Her clothes were not matching and she had not combed her hair. She **apologized**, saying, "I'm looking crazy right now." Rich said, "that's the hook!" and started singing those words. They knew they had found what they needed.

Guest stars

A lot of talented musicians appear on Beyoncé's solo album. Big Boi from Outkast features in "Hip Hop Star". Dancehall star Sean Paul appears on "Baby Boy". Hip-hop queen Missy Elliott and soul legend Luther Vandross are also guest stars.

Mathew's song

There is a track on *Dangerously in Love* that does not appear on the album's list of songs. It starts playing 15 seconds after the last song. It is a **tribute** by Beyoncé to her father.

Sean Paul and Missy Elliott both appear on *Dangerously in Love.*

tribute special way of thanking or remembering someone

Solo hits

Dangerously in Love was very well received. There were lots of different types of songs on the album. There were funky songs you could dance to. There were **ballads** and love songs. There was hip-hop and soul. Even though people had not liked lots of different styles on the first Destiny's Child album, they knew Beyoncé now and wanted to hear her songs. After "Crazy in Love", Beyoncé had hits with the singles "Baby Boy", "Me, Myself and I", and "Naughty Girl".

The Fighting Temptations

Beyoncé had her third acting part, *The Fighting Temptations*, in 2003. She appeared with actor Cuba Gooding Jr. She plays a jazz singer who joins a gospel choir to help them win a singing competition.

Beyoncé with Cuba Gooding Jr in the film *The Fighting Temptations*.

Star words   ballad slow and often sad song

On tour

Later in 2003, Beyoncé started her first solo tour in the UK. It was a **spectacular** show. In the opening sequence, she hangs upside down in a harness from the roof. She says, "It was actually my idea – I saw it in a Broadway show and it looked really cool." Early in 2004, Beyoncé toured the United States with Missy Elliott and Alicia Keys.

Award winner

Then came all the awards. In February 2004, Beyoncé won five Grammy awards. This is the most important award for music in the United States, so it was a major achievement. She opened the award show by performing with legendary musician Prince. She also had success at the Billboard Awards, the Brits, BET, the Video Music Awards, and MTV Europe awards.

Grammy star

Beyoncé was stunned to win so many Grammy awards. "This is unbelievable," she said. "Performing was enough for me. I'm just so honoured."

Beyoncé with her five Grammy awards.

⭐ Star fact

Beyoncé is not the only female musician to win five Grammy awards in one year. Lauryn Hill, Alicia Keys, and Norah Jones have also achieved this.

spectacular amazing or exciting

Behind the scenes

★ ★ ★ ★ ★ ★ ★ ★ ★ ★

Faith

Religion is an important part of Beyoncé's life. She and her family are Christians. She says that she has God to thank for her success. "God is the main person in my life and I would never do anything to offend Him."

★ ★ ★ ★ ★ ★ ★ ★ ★ ★

Beyoncé has become a very famous and very wealthy young woman. She has a lot of talent and has been very successful. She has achieved a lot, but there is still a lot that she wants to do. She says: "When I was young, my ambition was to get a recording deal and get a gold record and write a number one single. That was the only thing I wanted … But as soon as you **accomplish** one thing, it's not enough."

Responsibilities

Beyoncé admits that she is very driven and very focused, and has been since she was very young. Maybe she missed out on having a childhood, but it was her choice.

Beyoncé has fans hoping for autographs wherever she goes.

Star words   accomplish achieve

She says, "I've had the responsibility since I was 15 of someone who is 25 or 30, so now I have a lot of pressure … that has forced me to grow up a little faster."

The downside

Beyoncé is grateful to her fans, but admits that being famous has its downside. "Along with the good come all these people who want something from you … I just feel that there's certain things I can't control any more," she says.

A bodyguard has to follow Beyoncé to keep her safe.

Time off

Beyoncé likes to spend her spare time writing songs and painting. "I always have to do something creative or I'll go crazy," she says. She also likes to relax at home, "with no make-up on, with slippers on and watching television and eating chocolate ice cream."

Beyoncé or Sasha?

Beyoncé has a very sexy image, but she says that when she performs she turns into a character called "Sasha". "When I go up on stage being sexy, that's not me, that's her [Sasha] … so for that half an hour I'm on stage, I'm a completely different person."

Love and romance

Beyoncé has always been a private person. She does not like to discuss who she is dating or who she is involved with. When you are as famous as she is, however, the **media** will always try to find out what is going on in your life. She finds this difficult, but she accepts that it comes with the job.

> I have always tried to keep my personal life separate.

Beyoncé is well known for her sexy dance routines.

First love

Beyoncé met her first boyfriend, Lindell, when she was 12 years old. They went out until she was eighteen. After that, once her music career took off, dating was quite hard because she was so busy. "Having a music career doesn't allow for much of a social life," she admits.

Beyoncé and Jay-Z

Although she does her best to keep her private life private, Beyoncé's involvement with Jay-Z put them both in the spotlight. They have been seen out together at basketball games and at restaurants. They have appeared on each other's songs and in each other's videos. However, Jay-Z is just as keen as Beyoncé to keep his romances private. Neither of them want to talk to the media about whether they are dating or not.

★ Star fact

Beyoncé has many famous admirers. Prince William is said to be one of her fans!

All about Jay-Z

Jay-Z (above) was born in Brooklyn, New York in 1969. His first album, *Reasonable Doubt*, came out in 1996. He has had huge success as a rapper. He runs the record label Roc-A-Fella with Damon Dash and also has a very successful clothing line, called Roca Wear.

Emergency outfits

In 2000, Destiny's Child sang at President Bush's **inauguration**. Somehow, their costumes for the show got lost. Tina rushed out to buy new outfits, but security stopped her getting back in. The girls decided to cut up the t-shirts and trousers they had on and safety pin them back together. People loved the outfits and no one realized it was all a mistake!

Beyoncé and Tina often go to events in glamorous outfits.

Style and image

Beyoncé's career has always been a family affair. Her father is her **manager**. Her cousin, Angie, is her assistant. Her mother, Tina, has also had an important part to play in Beyoncé's success. She works as Destiny's Child's **stylist**. She also works with Beyoncé on her image as a solo artist.

Tina's style

When Destiny's Child were first starting out, they had very little money to spend on clothes. Tina used to make their outfits by hand. She became very good at taking cheap clothes and making them look amazing enough to wear on stage.

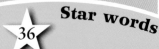
Star words

inauguration   special event marking the beginning of a US president's term of office

Shoes

Beyoncé loves high-heeled shoes. Tina says that her wardrobe is filled with more than one hundred pairs. She can also dance in shoes that many women could not even walk in.

★ Star fact

One of Mathew's rules for Destiny's Child is that the girls never wear the same thing twice when they are doing **promotional work**. Afterwards, their outfits are given to charity.

The Supremes were a girl-group in the 1960s.

Looking like stars

Tina wanted the girls to look classy and glamorous. She liked the look of female **Motown** stars of the 1960s such as The Supremes. They wore beautiful dresses and always looked stylish. When the girls were on stage, singing and dancing, she made them funky outfits that were fun and sassy.

Motown record label that released popular music by African American singers in the 1960s

Like J-Lo?

Many people have compared Beyoncé with Jennifer Lopez (below). What does Beyoncé think? She says she is flattered and that she respects J-Lo. However, she would rather not be compared to anyone else.

Beyoncé the business woman

Sometimes it seems that Beyoncé never stops working. Apart from her music and her acting, she has also set up her own fashion business with her mother Tina. They work closely together to design the clothes. The fashion company is called The House of Dereon. It makes two lines of clothes. One is casual – t-shirts and jeans. The other is more formal – elegant dresses and evening wear. The clothes were available to buy from autumn 2005.

Making money

Beyoncé has also made a lot of money **endorsing** different products. She is the face of a hair product company. She appeared in a soft-drink advert with fellow pop stars Britney Spears and Pink.

★ Star fact

Other hip-hop stars with clothing lines include Missy Elliott, Sean Combs, Jay-Z, Russell Simmons, Mike D of the Beastie Boys, and the Wu-Tang Clan.

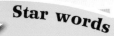
Star words

endorse when a famous person helps to advertise a product

She is also the face of a perfume. It is said that Beyoncé was paid £2 million for just one day's work on this advert!

> When you're a star, you should look like a star.
> (Tina Knowles)

Tina Knowles is using her fashion sense to help Beyoncé with her clothing line.

Madonna the mastermind

Beyoncé says that she admires Madonna (above), both for her music and because she is "a **mastermind** of the music business". She likes the way Madonna has always tried to turn negative events into positive ones. She says she tries to do that, too.

mastermind someone who is very clever and in control

Destiny's women

Talented trio

The girls had enjoyed their time apart, but they were glad to be together again. Recording the album was a positive time for everyone. Beyoncé says, "The chemistry was there right away. It was so refreshing to be in the room with two other talented people."

★ ★ ★ ★ ★ ★ ★ ★ ★ ★

In 2004 Destiny's Child were reunited. They started working together on a new album. The first single "Lose My Breath" was released in September. The album itself was released in November. It was called *Destiny Fulfilled*. A second single, called "Soldier", was released in the same month. In December, the girls had more good news. They received a Grammy nomination for Best R&B Vocal Performance by a Duo or Group. This was for the song "Lose My Breath".

Before splitting up again in 2005, the group went on a world tour, called "Destiny's Fulfilled … and Lovin' It". They visited 75 venues in 16 countries in just 5 months.

The group did lots of **promotional work** for their 2004 album.

Star words   collaborate work together

Kelly's hits

The other women of Destiny's Child had also been busy. Kelly's solo album *Simply Deep* had done well. She had hits with the songs "Stole" and "Can't Nobody". She also **collaborated** with hip-hop star Nelly on the hit song "Dilemma". They won a Grammy for the song in 2003.

> Through the past 3 years, we've grown... we've experienced love, heartache, heartbreak. (Michelle)

Michelle's work

Michelle had released two solo albums. Her first one, *Heart To Yours*, was an album of gospel music. Her second one was called *Do You Know*. She had also appeared on Broadway in the lead role of the musical *Aida*. Legendary musician Elton John wrote the music for this show.

Kelly the actress

Kelly had done some acting, too. She was in the horror film *Freddy vs Jason* (above) in 2003. She says it was "quite an experience, 'cause I don't even like horror movies. I was terrified on the set".

Beyoncé proudly shows off her programme to *Aida* starring Michelle Williams.

PLAYBILL

41

Bono of U2 was another famous face at the Nelson Mandela benefit concert.

What is next?

So what is next for Beyoncé? She loves making music and is not going to be retiring any time soon. She has said that she would like to try writing songs for other people.

> I want to continue to write classic songs that people will be hearing for the rest of their lives.

More acting

She also wants to carry on acting. In 2006, she appeared in the film *The Pink Panther* with Steve Martin and Kevin Kline. This film is a **prequel** to the famous comedies of the 1970s and 1980s starring Peter Sellers as Inspector Clouseau. She plays a pop star called Xania who may also be a murderer.

Working for charity

Beyoncé likes to give something back. She appeared at a major AIDS **benefit** in South Africa in 2003. The former president of South Africa, Nelson Mandela, organized this event. Beyoncé also **donated** money from her 2003 tour to the AIDS charity.

Beyoncé on the set of *The Pink Panther*.

Star words

benefit   concert held to raise money for charity
donate   give

This waxwork model of Beyoncé is on show at Madame Tussauds.

There are also rumours that Beyoncé will star in a film of her own life.

A family of her own?

Beyoncé has always been close to her family. Eventually she wants a family of her own. She says, "I want to work hard now so I can settle down in a few years and commit everything to my family and husband and hopefully kids. I'm working now so I can rest later."

Salaries
for films

The Fighting Temptations
US#1.5 million

Austin Powers in
Goldmember
US#3 million

prequel film that is based on another film. It tells an earlier story and is the opposite of a sequel.

Find out more

Books

Beyoncé, Kathleen Tracy
 (Mitchell Lane Publishers, 2005)
*Destiny's Style – Bootylicious Fashion, Beauty,
 and Lifestyle Secrets from Destiny's Child*,
 Tina Knowles with Zoe Alexander
 (Regan Books, 2002)
*Soul Survivors, the Official Autobiography of
 Destiny's Child*, Beyoncé Knowles, Kelly
 Rowland, and Michelle Williams, with James
 Patrick Herman (Boxtree, 2002)

Discography

Destiny Fulfilled, 2004 (with Destiny's Child)
Dangerously in Love, 2003
This is the Remix, 2002 (with Destiny's Child)
Survivor, 2001 (with Destiny's Child)
8 Days of Christmas, 2001 (with Destiny's Child)
The Writing's on the Wall, 1999
 (with Destiny's Child)
Destiny's Child, 1998 (with Destiny's Child)

Filmography

The Pink Panther, 2006
The Fighting Temptations, 2003
Austin Powers in Goldmember, 2002
Carmen: A Hip Hopera, 2001

Websites

To find out more about Beyoncé and Destiny's Child, try these websites:

www.destinyschild.com
www.beyonceonline.com

Another good music website is:

www.bbc.co.uk/totp

Disclaimer

All the Internet addresses (URLs) given in this book were valid at the time of going to press. However, due to the dynamic nature of the Internet, some addresses may have changed, or sites may have ceased to exist since publication. While the author and publishers regret any inconvenience this may cause readers, no responsibility for any such changes can be accepted by either the author or the publishers.

Glossary

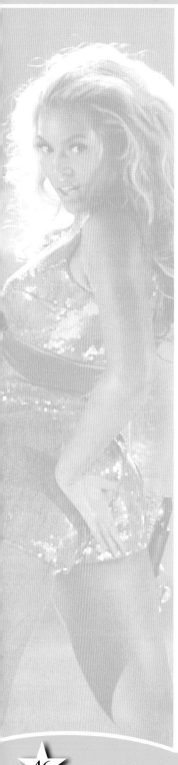

a cappella singing without any instruments or music

accomplish achieve

apologize say that you are sorry for something

ASCAP American Society of Composers, Authors and Publishers

audition chance for a musician or actor to perform to see if they are right to join a group or get a part

ballad slow and often sad song

benefit concert held to raise money for charity

chaperone person who looks after and supervises younger people

collaborate work together

committed very serious about something

contribute give

debut first

depression unhappiness

dermatologist doctor who works on skin problems

devastated very sad and upset

devious dishonest

director person in charge of making a film

diva famous woman who is thought to be bossy and demanding

donate give

endorse when a famous person helps to advertise a product

executive business person

inauguration special event marking the beginning of a US president's term of office

inherit passed down from your parents or grandparents

legal guardian someone who is not your real parent, but who is responsible for looking after you

lip-synch mime the words to a song rather than singing them

maiden name woman's surname before she is married

manager person that takes care of the business side of running a pop group

mastermind someone who is very clever and in control

media types of communication such as television, radio, newspapers, and magazines

Motown record label that released popular music by African American singers in the 1960s

pageant show or competition

prequel film that is based on another film. It tells an earlier story and is the opposite of a sequel.

producer person that decides how a song will sound when it is being recorded

promotional work appearing on television and radio shows to talk about a new song, album, film etc

publicity attention from newspapers, magazines, television and radio shows

rehearse practise for a musical or acting performance

spectacular amazing or exciting

stylist person who gives advice on hair, clothes, and make-up

transformed completely changed

tribute special way of thanking or remembering someone

Index

Titles in the *Star File* series include:

Johnny Depp
Jane Bingham

Hardback   1 844 43283 1

Beyoncé Knowles
Mark Stewart

Hardback   1 844 43296 3

Jackie Chan
Dan Fox

Hardback   1 844 43295 5

Usher
Dan Whitcombe

Hardback   1 844 43298 X

David Beckham
Paul Harrison

Hardback   1 844 43297 1

Andre Benjamin
Brian Fitzgerald

Hardback   1 844 43972 0

Mary-Kate and Ashley Olsen
Stephanie Fitzgerald

Hardback   1 410 91662 6

Orlando Bloom
Kay Barnham

Hardback   1 844 43284 X

Find out about other titles in this series on our website www.raintreepublishers.co.uk